WARNING!
Things That Can Destroy Your New York Car Accident Case

(And the Insurance Companies Already Know These Things)

WARNING!
Things That Can Destroy Your New York Car Accident Case

(And the Insurance Companies Already Know These Things)

Gary E. Rosenberg

Law Offices of
GARY E. ROSENBERG, P.C.

109-05 72nd Road
Forest Hills, NY 11375
Telephone: (718) 520-8787
www.InjuryAtty.net
www.RealEstateAtty.net

Printed in the United States of America.

ISBN 10: 1-59571-171-6
ISBN 13: 978-1-59571-171-7
Library of Congress Control Number: 2006938862

Word Association Publishers
205 5th Avenue
Tarentum, PA 15084
www.wordassociation.com

The insurance industry is driving a stake through the heart of your automobile accident case, and the courts are swinging the mallet. I wrote this book to help accident victims get justice. I've learned the ins and outs of accident cases over the years, and I share them with you here. Hopefully, you'll find this little book useful.

I have been practicing law since 1983. My firm, the Law Offices of Gary E. Rosenberg, P.C., mostly represents people injured in accidents. I have offices in Queens (Forest Hills) and Brooklyn, New York, and represent injured people throughout the Greater New York metropolitan area, including the five boroughs of the City of New York, Long Island (Nassau and Suffolk) and Westchester, Rockland and Duchess counties. I am devoted to getting justice for injured persons from insurance companies.

Now what do I mean by that last sentence? It is my belief that insurance companies exist to collect peoples' premium dollars, but that they hate to pay claims. Every year insurance companies get stingier and stingier. They're always looking to try to save money, or cut down on what they consider fraud, and so forth. There is never a year where insurance company claims departments are told to make generous payments to legitimately injured persons. Insurance company investigators are out there hiding behind bushes and trees and conducting surveillance to try to catch injured claimants engaged in activities that they claim to be unable to do. There is no "justice" from insurance companies; they do not care about playing fair. Insurance companies increase profits by decreasing the amount of money they pay out in claims.

I have written this book for people injured in accidents or who know people who are injured in accidents or who just want to learn a little about what is a very confusing area of New York State law. As you read on, you'll find a lot of stuff to think about. Hopefully, you'll also think of some questions, because this little book is too limited to answer all possible questions about this very specialized area of the law. Maybe you'll ask questions of an attorney. Most important, I want to emphasize that this book is not meant to give legal advice and nothing in this book is legal advice. However, I hope it will get you thinking.

The most common kind of accident is a motor vehicle accident. Maybe involving two cars, or a car and a truck, or a car and a pedestrian, or a car and bicycle, or sometimes several vehicles. There are several common forms of motor vehicle accidents:

- The hit in the rear (the well known "rear-ender");

- The question of lights ("I had the green light." "No, you didn't. I had the green light");

- The left-turning car colliding with a car going straight;

- The side-swipe;

- The stop sign (no one ever seems to admit running a stop sign, they all say, "I stopped and looked and waited and proceeded slowly and carefully into the intersection and 'boom.' The other car was speeding and had its lights off and came out of nowhere.")

It is well known that cars are safer now; I can usually tell when a potential client has not worn his or her seatbelt in an accident, because that's when I see the worst injuries.

With safer cars, fewer people are getting injured catastrophically, fewer broken bones and the like. This makes the attorney's job harder, because an accident victim can still be crippled by a less obvious injury, which can be hard to diagnose. Also, cars are stronger and harder to break, so that there may be less visible evidence of property damage to the vehicles involved in an accident. This means there are fewer "easy" accident cases, and more cases are being turned down by attorneys that don't understand how to win a lawsuit for injuries that may be crippling, yet hard to prove.

From New York Newsday:

State law causing downturn

One reason is that cars are getting safer at the same time that the state's no-fault law is getting stricter, meaning injuries have to be more and more serious to justify a lawsuit. Under the no-fault law, a person must suffer a bone fracture, significant scar, dismemberment, major loss of movement, loss of function of a body part, or the death of a loved one to file a suit, lawyers said.

And appellate courts are tightening the definitions of such injuries all the time. For example, a scar used to have to be significant, but now it must be "shocking to the public." The stricter the law gets, the more potential clients' lawyers must turn away because their injuries won't pass muster in court.

The expense of hiring experts to testify - and the standards that expert testimony must meet to be admitted in court - rises every year. Many attorneys say they'll turn cases away because they would spend as much on expert witnesses and other research as they could hope to win in a settlement or award.

When all is said and done, it can cost $20,000 or $30,000 to pursue a case that's barely worth $20,000 or $30,000.

Autos are safer

In auto cases, air bags, child safety seats and more people buckling up all are keeping more people from getting seriously hurt. The fact that baby boomers have passed out of their hot-rodding years, but have not yet entered old age, doesn't hurt either, according to Robert Hartwig, chief economist for the Manhattan-based Insurance Information Institute, a trade group.

Hartwig said that nationally, the number of car accidents involving injuries dropped 37 percent from 1993 to 2003. The number of people killed in car accidents dropped 22 percent in that same period.

Why fewer are following suit

Some factors leading to the drop in personal injury lawsuits:

- Safer cars

- More disputes settled through mediation/arbitration

- Higher cost of hiring expert witnesses

- Stricter no-fault insurance laws, which raise the standard for filing lawsuits

- More motorists and passengers using seat belts

After a rise in the 1990s, the number of personal-injury lawsuits stemming from motor vehicle accidents declined in recent years.

Fewer lawsuits mean lawyers are fighting to get fewer cases. Unfortunately, many lawyers don't know how to handle accident cases.

What to expect the lawyer you hire for your auto accident case to do.

- Gather evidence: photographs, police reports, witness statements.

- Determine insurance coverages available to protect client.

- File No-Fault insurance and uninsured/underinsured motorist claim forms (within thirty days of accident).

- If necessary, file claim with Motor Vehicle Accident Indemnification Corporation (MVAIC).

- Prepare client for insurance company's No-Fault medical examinations.

- Notify and prepare client for Examination Under Oath (EUO) and/or municipal "50-h" (statutory) hearing.

- If applicable, advise client about disability benefits, lost wage benefits, Workers' Compensation benefits.

- Obtain hospital and physicians' records.

- Send medical reports to insurance company to try to settle.

- If case doesn't settle, commence lawsuit or demand arbitration.

- Fight lawsuit. Engage in discovery (or sharing information with the other side), Examination Before Trial (EBT), etc. Prepare client for defendant's medical examinations. Seek information from defendant. Provide information to defendant as demanded (and as may be proper).

- Place case on court's trial calendar.

- Make and defend any motions (applications to the judge).

- Organize and prepare for trial. Keep updating client's medical records.

- Trial through verdict, including preparing and presenting medical witnesses (doctors) and fact witnesses.

- If unhappy with result, analyze case for possible appeal (generally not included in basic retainer).

DID YOU KNOW THAT THERE IS A CLIENT "BILL OF RIGHTS"? Every New York attorney is required to hang this list of rights in his or her office – where clients can read it. The complete list of ten items is at the back of this book, in Appendix "A."

Human Anatomy

The most common injury occurs from the bouncing around of a body in a vehicle. Often, a car occupant's neck "whips" back and forth, giving rise to what is known as an acceleration-deceleration injury, or the often maligned "whiplash."

In acceleration injury the head is put into motion from a stand still position, as a result of which the different layers of the brain travel at different velocities with shearing effects and rotation of the brain within the skull. This is seen in motor vehicle accidents where the car is hit from the back. In deceleration injury the head it brought to a stand still from a moving position as it falls. Since the head is a large weight on the neck, the neck takes the brunt of the force.

Frequently, the lower back is hurt, as well. Occasionally someone slams a knee into the dashboard or breaks a pinky, but these types of injuries are not common.

1. What is a "soft tissue" injury? Put simply, a soft tissue injury is one where no bones are broken. Soft tissue injury is the most common type of accident injury. Whiplash is one type of soft

tissue injury. Often an accident victim can be badly hurt, but may not feel it immediately. Some people get gradually worse.

2. I've had clients come into my office after an accident, and they seemed pain-free, able to twist and bend, and converse with me easily. Then they get worse and worse and may need surgery. I've also had clients come in after an accident in great discomfort. Wearing one of those padded collars around their necks; having trouble sitting down in the chair in my office. Having trouble standing up. I've accepted cases like that and seen people get all better. The point is that you never know if you're going to heal. I don't know if you're going to heal. Even the doctors don't really know if you're going to heal. Usually, only "time will tell."

3. Soft tissue injuries generally refer to the spine: the neck and back. The spinal cord is approximately $1\frac{1}{2}$ feet long, round, slightly thicker than a pencil, and goes from the base of the brain to the tail bone (sacrum). It supports the body. In addition to allowing the body to remain upright and flex and twist, the spinal cord acts like a large electrical cable with smaller cables (nerves) running inside it, and

branching out into the arms, legs and other parts of the body; imagine, if you will, a tree and its branches.

4. The spine is constructed of bones known as vertebrae. But if the spine was solid bone, it could not bend and twist. Therefore, in addition to being wrapped in muscles and ligaments and such, the bones or vertebrae are separated by, held together by, and sandwiched between, discs. These are soft, shock-absorber-like structures. Harder on the outside and softer on the inside; imagine, if you will, a jelly donut. Every spinal vertebra (bone) has a number, and the spinal discs each have two numbers — like an address – of the two vertebrae on either side of it. For example, the disc in the cervical spine (neck) between spinal vertebra C1 and spinal vertebra C2 is known as C1-C2.

5. The nerves run through and in and out of the spine. The nerves transmit nerve impulses (electrical-like signals) that move muscles in the body. Closest to the spine are the nerve roots.

6. Nerves and discs are the anatomical structures we most often refer to when discussing spinal injuries. Less frequently involved are ligaments and muscles. Ligaments are bands of tough

tissue that connect bones and hold them in place. Ligaments generally get injured when stretched. This is called a "sprain" which generally heals. Muscles move the spine.

Soft Tissue Injuries

1. The holy grail of soft tissue injuries is the herniated disc. Its first cousin is the bulging disc. Simply put, a bulging disc injury occurs when the shape of the disc changes so that part of the disc bulges outside its usual boundaries between the spinal vertebrae. A herniated disc is more severe; the soft material inside the disc bulges out also, and may leak. Imagine, if you will, squeezing a jelly donut so that it starts to ooze. Note: Not all disc herniations hurt. And you can have pain without a disc herniation. Pain may come and go; many people have good days and bad days.

2. These types of injuries are bad for two reasons.

   First, over time the injured disc can lose its flexibility and ability to cushion the spinal vertebrae. This could lead to rubbing and irritation, and maybe arthritis between the vertebrae. Very bad.

Second, the spine is a miracle of engineering – there's not a lot of extra space anywhere. So a bulging or herniated disc frequently moves against something, and that something is commonly a nerve root. This can irritate the nerve root and prevent it from functioning correctly. In extreme cases the nerve root can die. This can lead to pain, numbness, muscle weakness and a host of other problems.

Another type of spinal nerve injury: through the spine's movement and whipping back and forth the nerve root gets "pinched" by one of the anatomical structures next to it.

These nerve injuries are sometimes referred to as radiculopathy or radiculitis.

3. An important concept when considering spinal injuries is "dermatomes." This refers to the levels of the spine and nerves and what areas of the body they serve. For instance, the part of the spine closer to the head (commonly known as the cervical spine), has nerves that branch out and run into the shoulders, arms and fingers. Thus, a neck injury may lead to tingling or pain in your shoulder, arms, or fingers. A fracture of the spine at the cervical level that damages the

spinal cord may cause a loss of function at or below that area. So that such an injury may cause paralysis of the arms and legs. The part of the spine closer to the tail bone (commonly known as the lumbar spine) has nerves that branch through your buttocks and down your legs to your feet. Thus a lumbar spine injury may lead to tingling or pain down your legs. A fracture of the lumbar spine may disable all the nerves beneath that level, so that a person might suffer paralysis and an inability to walk, but still have perfect arm and hand function.

4. At the back of this book, in Appendix "B", there are medical drawings showing the anatomy of the spine and a herniated disc. There are two different views. A cutaway side view and a cutaway view looking down. These drawings show the herniated disc material leaking out of the disc and impinging (or crushing) the nerve root. Please look at them. I guarantee that you will find the drawings helpful in understanding this most common type of soft-tissue spine injury.

Diagnostic Tools

Proving soft tissue injury to the satisfaction of a judge or jury or, more likely, an insurance company, is no simple matter. A person may legitimately hurt, but documenting the injury can be difficult and expensive. Without a fracture or broken bones, x-rays are of no use. They won't show soft tissue injury. Soft tissue injuries don't bleed (you can't put a band-aid on them).

The biggest problem is that soft tissue injuries have a bad reputation. They are easy to claim and hard to prove. It is easy for a healthy person to say, "My back hurts," or "My neck hurts," which is, unfortunately, too common. This makes it harder for persons actually injured to recover fair monetary damages. These injuries are also maligned in the press, often as part of insurance company propaganda. We've all seen television exposés of persons claiming injuries that get caught on video tape doing heavy physical labor. Rarely do we see the person crippled by a soft tissue neck or back injury, who can't get just compensation, can't put food on the table or can't pay the rent.

Here's a secret you should know: Justice does not always prevail. The truth does not always win in court. If a lie is proven, a lie can win and an injured accident victim can lose!

How do we prove soft tissue injury?

I told you that x-rays do not show soft tissue injury. However, they may show changes to the shape of the spine (which is bone) caused by muscle spasm. Generally, however, x-rays are of little use in showing soft tissue injury. A CT scan or CAT scan is a 3-D x-ray, and also of little use in diagnosing soft tissue injury.

Commonly used to show herniated or bulging discs is: Magnetic Resonance Imaging or MRI. Rather than using radiation, the MRI uses a magnetic field to show soft tissue – muscle, ligaments, and organs. Insurance companies do not like to pay for MRI testing, because it's expensive. **Here's a secret**: Some doctors like MRI tests because. . . they're expensive. Beware of medical facilities that over-test with MRIs following an accident. Some unscrupulous facilities will send an automobile accident patient for too, too many MRIs, for every imaginable body part. Insurance companies pick up on this rather quickly, and the damage to the reputation of that doctor or facility may hurt your lawsuit. On the other hand, if you have pain in your neck or back that doesn't go away, and especially if you have nerve-type shooting pains (remember: radiculopathy or radiculitis) you may want to make certain that your doctor does send you for an MRI of the affected body part. At the minimum, this is something that you may want to discuss with your physician.

Another secret: A problem with MRIs is that they are subject to interpretation. That means that one specialist (a radiologist) can read an MRI film and see a serious accident-related soft-tissue injury while another radiologist – typically hired by an insurance company to defend a lawsuit – may see no injury, or an old, pre-existing injury, or nothing much at all: just degenerative changes due to the passage of time and wear-and-tear on the body, but nothing accident-related.

A test often used to test for nerve damage is the electromyogram (electromyography) or EMG test. Once you have an EMG test you won't forget it. The EMG requires insertion of needles into your muscles. EMG uses tiny electrical impulses to test for nerve root injury. It may not say why the nerve is injured – that comes from other tests and your doctor's clinical experience, as well as your medical history.

Other tests are range of motion (ROM) tests – the ability to move, bend or twist your neck or back and muscle strength studies. While low-tech and usually not involving the use of any special equipment, ROM tests have taken on great importance in the area of auto accident cases, as will be shown at greater length below.

Once these soft-tissue injuries are proven to exist, the next hurdle is proving they were caused by the accident, and not by some prior incident, accident, medical condition, or disease.

Treatment

What kind of treatment can you expect for your soft tissue injury?

Common treatments:

- Traction
- Physical therapy – applied stretching and strength-building exercises
- Cryotherapy: apply ice or cold
- Heat
- Massage
- Injections into points of spasm
- Low voltage electric stimulation

- Medication (muscle relaxers/anti-inflammatories)
- Biofeedback
- Conservative treatment - bed rest, analgesics, a cervical collar
- Chiropractic care: can include massage, heat, electrical stimulation, etc.
- Surgery: a last resort

The New York "No-Fault" Law

Some thoughts on injuries in car accidents. Insurance companies try to sell the idea that if there is not a lot of damage to your car, you can't be seriously hurt. This has been disproved by numerous studies, but let me tell you about a demonstration that some attorneys have used at trial to demonstrate injury to the jury. A low speed car accident can push your body and brain back and forth, even without a lot of property damage. **A good lawyer trick:** A trial attorney may hold up and drop a carton of eggs to the ground. The eggs break, yet the carton remains visibly undamaged. Like the eggs, the human body can be hurt, yet a car, like the egg carton, can show very little outside damage.

Insurance companies seem to have the attitude that everyone exaggerates or fakes pain. In thousands of negotiations with insurance companies, I've heard them "poo-poo" clients' complaints of pain. Pain alone won't carry the day, either for settlement, or in court. Learn why by reading on.

What do we mean by "No-Fault"?

Put simply, No-Fault refers to having your accident-related medical bills paid, up to $50,000, regardless of whose fault the accident is. Two different things happen after a car accident. First: No-Fault insurance pays your medical bills and lost wages, except in certain instances involving buses, motorcycles and heavy trucks. No-Fault also protects pedestrians and bicycle riders. This should not be confused with issues of liability in an accident, which are very much about who is at fault, and the focus of the second thing that may happen: a lawsuit. Let's learn about No-Fault insurance and what it means for your car accident case.

New York's No-Fault law was enacted on December 1, 1977 and is found at Article 51 of New York State's Insurance Law. Before the No-Fault statute, an accident victim could sue for any kind of injury and often did. The insurance industry wanted to cut down on the small strain and sprain cases that were flooding the courthouses and, hopefully, reduce auto insurance premiums, so it proposed a trade. Smaller cases would not be allowed to recover money damages, and in exchange, the insurance companies would pay medical bills for those injured in a car accident, regardless of fault – even if the injured person caused the accident. If this sounds simple, it is anything but.

The goal of the No-Fault law is to compensate for "basic economic loss" by paying medical bills and lost wages. Under No-Fault, in order to sustain a lawsuit for pain and suffering and such, you need what the No-Fault statute calls a "serious injury." "Serious injury" is rather an unfortunate phrase as it implies a greater level of injury than required. One lawyer-commentator has said that it would have been far better for accident victims if the statute referred to a "qualifying injury" instead of a "serious injury." The serious injury requirement is intended to keep smaller cases out of court, and is referred to as the No-Fault "threshold." Frequently, it is used by insurance companies to keep deserving cases out of court, and lawyers not thoroughly familiar with the ins and outs of the No-Fault threshold can lose these cases, even when they shouldn't.

You should not be surprised if I tell you that insurance companies are cheap with No-Fault insurance benefits: even though No-Fault benefits are supposed to help the injured person, and the injured person is less able to bring a court case because of the No-Fault law. In many cases, the insurance companies nit-pick the amount of doctors' bills submitted under the No-Fault law or refuse to pay them for no good reason. The insurance carriers may send out an accident victim's medical records for "peer review," where a doctor that has never examined or even met the injured person recommends denying treatment as "unnecessary." Insurance companies are also quick to cancel No-Fault insurance benefits, which they are permitted to do after they hire a physician to examine the accident victim, if that physician finds that continued treatment would not benefit the accident victim. Would it shock you to learn that these physicians, paid by the insurance carriers, overwhelmingly find that further treatment is unnecessary and/or that the injured person is able to return to work, thus justifying the discontinuance of No-Fault insurance benefits? Ironically, these insurance carrier-sponsored physicals are called "Independent Medical Examinations" – they are certainly not "independent."

How the No-Fault serious injury threshold works.

To recover non-economic loss damages and sue in a civil action, the injured person must establish that he or she satisfies the requirements of the No-Fault law. The No-Fault law precludes recovery for pain and suffering, between "covered persons," unless the accident victim proves a "serious injury." This is one of the most litigated sections of New York law, with many, many reported case decisions.

Now remember, we are not even talking about liability or fault for the accident, which is a separate issue entirely. We are only talking about the degree of injury.

The nine No-Fault serious injuries in New York State's Insurance Law are:

1. Death (brought about by the accident);
2. Dismemberment – mangling, mutilation or dismemberment (loss of) a body part;
3. Significant disfigurement (a scar; there's no hard and fast formula for scar size – depends on the visibility of the scar; usually scars above scalp line don't clear the threshold) ;
4. A fracture (broken bone);
5. Loss of a fetus (traumatic abortion);
6. Permanent loss of use of a body organ, member, function or system (the first of the "tricky" categories);
7. Permanent consequential limitation of use of a body organ or member (pain alone won't do; headaches alone won't do; a herniated/bulging disc alone won't do; sprains/strains won't do);
8. Significant limitation of use of a body function or system; or,
9. A medically determined injury or impairment of a non-permanent nature

which prevents the injured person from performing substantially all of the material acts which constitute such person's usual and customary daily activities for not less than ninety days during the one hundred eighty days immediately following the occurrence of the injury or impairment (known as the 90 out of 180 days rule).

The first five are the easy categories, they are fairly straightforward.

The two less tricky categories:

Number 6: If you can no longer use a part of your body, you can qualify.

Number 9: Usual and customary daily activities generally means that you miss three months of work in the first six months after the accident, but there are two wrinkles. First: Your failure to work has to be medically determined. In other words, your doctor must say that you can't work. Second: You need to show that you couldn't do any of your other customary daily activities. This may be housework, driving the children to school, or other things.

The two trickier categories:

Numbers 7 and 8 have no fixed definition or explanation. Some cases make it; some don't. Your lawyer needs a thorough understanding of the current case law to know how the courts are applying these two threshold categories. Frequently, it comes down to documenting a reduced range of motion in the injured part of your body – for example the doctor determines that you can't fully bend or twist or turn your back or neck. I have more to say about these two categories as you read on.

How defendants use the No-Fault serious injury threshold to destroy your case.

When you sue someone for injuries from an automobile accident, the insurance company or companies for the people you are suing hire a law firm to protect the defendants by fighting the lawsuit. There are two ways that they can beat you with the No-Fault threshold.

First: The defense can ask the judge, on papers, to throw out your case. This defense application to the judge is called a "motion" and, more particularly, a summary judgment motion. Since this is all done on paper, there is no testimony given in court and, while your doctors will be asked to give evidence on paper – in the form of affidavits – neither the injured person (sometimes called the "plaintiff") nor the doctors have to appear at the courthouse.

If you lose this motion, your case is thrown out – even though you've never been heard by a jury. Perhaps the largest body of case law in New York today consists of decisions on these summary judgment motions seeking to apply the No-Fault threshold to throw out cases brought by automobile accident victims.

Second: The injured person may win the summary judgment motion, or the defense may not bother making one. However, you then win only the right to have a jury hear your claim. After trial, either the jury or the judge (again) can throw out your case if the injuries you sustain do not breach the serious injury threshold.

WHAT YOU SHOULD KNOW:

Many lawyers don't "get it" and will turn down your case if you don't have a broken bone (fracture). So you may have a broken pinky or broken toe that heals perfectly and a lawyer will gladly take your case, even though the injury may only be worth a few dollars – the lawyer who doesn't understand the No-Fault serious injury threshold may see easy dollars. Far more difficult is the case of the accident victim who is unable to work due to crippling back pain, with no fracture. How does that person prove a serious injury?

More important details about how defendants use the No-Fault serious injury threshold to destroy your case.

1. Attached at the end of this book as Appendix "C" there is a beautiful sample of a physician's affidavit used by my firm, in an actual lawsuit, to beat a defense summary judgment motion based on the No-Fault serious injury threshold. If you have a lawsuit with soft tissue injuries, I urge you to show a copy of this sample doctors' affidavit to your attorney, so she can get an idea of one lawyer's approach (mine) to beating the defense summary judgment motion.

2. In making a motion to have your case thrown out based on your failure to prove a serious injury, the defense has the initial burden of showing to the court that you are not injured. At trial, the opposite is true, and

the burden is on the injured person to come forward and show the injury.

3. The evidence submitted by both sides (plaintiff fighting against the summary judgment motion and defendant fighting for the summary judgment motion) must be sworn to under oath (notarized); except under certain circumstances the defense can use unsworn medical reports and, in that instance, the plaintiff can also rely on those reports without the necessity of having them sworn to. Just so you know, licensed physicians (but not chiropractors) can use an "affirmation" which is considered sworn to, even though it doesn't have to be notarized. For purposes of this little book, you may consider an affidavit as the same as an affirmation.

4. Any doctor's opinion must be based on a fairly recent examination.

5. An affidavit from an attorney is accorded little weight and is fairly useless.

6. **A case killer:** Long lapses (interruptions) in treatment by the injured person. If you have a long lapse in treatment, you better have a good explanation. The only excuse that

seems to work is that a doctor says that treatment was not doing you any good, and maybe you were given exercises to do at home, so there was no sense in continued treatment. This is a risky argument, at best. Don't even try this argument unless your doctor will swear in an affidavit that you, the injured person, was given this medical advice.

7. **A case helper:** If your vehicle has suffered a lot of damage and you have photographs: use them. One picture is worth a thousand words and gruesome photos of your car, all mangled, may create the impression that you, as an occupant of that vehicle, probably got tossed around pretty good. (This is not really a contradiction to what I said before about how you can be injured in an accident where there's little damage to the car, because severe damage to the car always looks better to the judge, the jury and, yes, an insurance carrier.)

8. Some thoughts about getting property damage photographs of your vehicle.

   a. Get them as soon as possible after the accident; before the vehicle is repaired. Don't count on your garage or insurance company to take photographs or, if they do, that they will share copies with you.

b. Shoot many photographs, from different angles, distances and positions. If you use film that needs to be developed (not a digital camera), get it developed immediately and before the car is repaired to make sure your photos came out. Once the car is fixed – it's too late. If you use a digital camera, make sure the photos are good. Make sure the license plates show in some of the photos.

c. Look for hidden damage to the vehicle. If your car took a hard hit in the rear, sometimes the inside of the trunk is pushed in. The frame of the car may be bent. If there's damage to the inside of the car, get photographs: of deflated airbags, glass scattered in the inside of the car, a collapsed seat, a broken dashboard, etc.

d. It may be especially difficult to get photographs if you were a passenger in someone else's car. Try to get photos anyway.

9. If you have had more than one accident it's best if you have the same doctor and the same lawyer. Sometimes accident victims think they'll get more money if they keep their accidents separate and secret from their lawyer and doctors. This is a recipe for disaster because the insurance companies report all accident claims to a central computer. So they will know about all of your accidents. The only surprise will be to the team of professionals trying to help you. If you have more than one accident case, the doctor must be able to distinguish the injuries between the two accidents.

10. Similarly, if you have a pre-existing condition or disease that affects your treatment, you must tell your doctor. In defending a defense summary judgment motion to throw out your case for failure to reach the No-Fault serious injury threshold, your physician must be able to sort out your accident-related injuries from your pre-existing condition.

11. What about psychological injury? Generally this won't breach the No-Fault threshold. But maybe it can if it's disabling. You'd have to show ongoing treatment,

with medication. Depression from pain may work. Or Post Traumatic Stress Disorder (PTSD), but it would have to be severe. Usually, this kind of stress would accompany severe physical injury. I once represented a World War II Holocaust survivor who was severely injured in a car accident. Before the accident, she lived a fairly normal life as a housewife and had a fairly high level of functioning. The trauma of the accident brought this elderly woman back to the Holocaust, back to the concentration camps. She was so depressed she underwent electric shock therapy, which didn't help. Her case settled for a large amount of money. It's been said that pain that never stops is a window into hell. That's the level of difficulty you would have to demonstrate.

12. Concussion. You can get this from the whipping action of the neck, even without striking anything (*e.g.*, mirror, windshield, side column, dashboard). But it's difficult to prove.

13. TMJ – The TMJ joint connects the lower jaw to the skull. Usually diagnosed by a dentist, a sufferer may have jaw pain or jaw

clicking, difficulty chewing, and his or her mouth may lock open. This is difficult to treat. Some dentists make appliances for the mouth to correct the positioning of the jaw. In extreme cases, sufferers undergo surgery.

14. Headache. Alone won't do. And, anyway, difficult to prove.

15. Treatment by a chiropractor. Believed by many to be a case killer. I know, like, and respect many chiropractors, but the medical community and most juries just don't consider them "real" doctors. The smart chiropractor will partner with a medical doctor or two in treating an accident victim. Just chiropractic care alone usually won't breach the serious injury threshold. I have attorney friends that specialize in accident cases that won't take your case if your treatment is mostly by a chiropractor.

16. Economic damages. In serious cases the smart attorney may hire a vocational specialist and/or an economist to quantify the money lost over the accident victim's working life. This can be useful even with accident victims that are partially disabled, but can still work. In my experience, they

can't work as hard as they used to. They may lose out on promotions and overtime. Pension benefits may be smaller. In addition, the accident victim may miss work due to injury flare-ups or to attend doctor appointments. Worse, partially disabled accident victims are less likely to have job mobility (change jobs) because frequently their co-workers help them with physical tasks. They might not expect or receive such assistance at a new job. Thus, even returning to full duty with a partially disabling injury can cost you money over the course of your work life.

17. What other things are important? What the injured person can't do:

a. Social: dancing (wear high heels?); go to parties? Go out?

b. Athletics: walk/run/exercise: aerobics, softball, tennis, swimming, bowling, basketball. Maybe the accident victim can do these things a little bit, but not as long, strong, hard (intensely). Does the injured person have difficulty participating in kids' activities? Can he or she sleep on the ground in a tent on a scout camping trip?

Run around and coach soccer, or anything similar?

c. Chores: carry the groceries? Maybe only carry two bags instead of six. Carry laundry? Garden? Move furniture to clean floors? Paint? Reach the top shelf in the kitchen cupboard to get down a can of soup? Can you pick up your children? Your grandchildren? Can you lift and carry a baby to change a diaper?

d. The eventual onset of arthritis. Interrupted sleep. Pain due to changes in weather.

e. How does this make you feel? How's your mood? Despair?

18. Spousal loss of consortium or loss of services. The spouse of a married accident victim has a claim for the impact that the accident has on the marriage. Why not have the spouse put in an affidavit to oppose the defense summary judgment motion? Talk about the damage to the marital relationship. How the pain affects intimate relations, how pain makes the injured spouse want to stay home and not socialize

or participate in family outings, how the pain leads to moodiness and fights. How the spouse can't work or wakes up moaning in pain, waking the uninjured spouse. Does the uninjured spouse have to drive the accident victim to doctor appointments? Does s/he miss work because of this? Does the uninjured spouse have to do more chores around the house to compensate for the spouse's injuries? Carry more groceries, do the laundry alone? Does the uninjured spouse have to help care for the injured person? Give massages or help with hot showers or help administer medication? Rub the injured person with BenGay ointment? Bring a heating pad? Help the injured spouse tie his shoes or get dressed? How has the quality of the marriage deteriorated?

What do the Cases Say?

Some actual quotations from New York summary judgment cases may clarify the No-Fault serious injury threshold for you.

Accident victim loses. Defendant met his initial burden by establishing that plaintiff did not sustain a serious injury within the meaning of Insurance Law Section 5102(d). In opposition, the plaintiff failed to raise a triable issue of fact. The plaintiff's affidavit and the affirmations and affidavits of her experts failed to address the findings of degeneration in her spine as noted in the affirmed medical report of the defendant's examining radiologist, rendering speculative the findings that the injuries to her spine were caused by the subject accident. *Cardillo v. Xenakis.*

Accident victim loses. Where, as here, plaintiff sustained injuries as a result of accidents or incidents that preceded the accident giving rise to the litigation, plaintiff's expert must adequately address how plaintiff's current medical problems, in light of her past medical history, are causally related to the subject accident. This she failed to do. Of the four experts whose affirmations plaintiff submitted in opposition to the motion, only one mentioned plaintiff's medical history. In a conclusory manner, this expert stated that plaintiff had experienced "neck and back pain prior to the accident" and "was improving from [her preexisting] injuries" at the time of the subject accident. This expert then summarily concluded that, as a result of the subject accident, plaintiff's "condition became more severe and required a return to regular therapy." Given plaintiff's medical history, this explanation was inadequate to raise a triable issue of fact as to whether plaintiff's current medical problems are causally related to the subject accident. Therefore, plaintiff failed to rebut defendant's prima facie showing of entitlement to judgment as a matter of law. *Style v. Joseph.*

Accident victim loses. While it is uncontested that Uddin missed three months of work within the first 180 days, his allegations do not mention any other daily activities that were substantially hindered due to the injury.

To the extent the affirmation in opposition by Dr. DiGiancinto, Uddin's treating neurosurgeon, noted deficiencies in the range of motion of his lumbar spine, such findings were secondary to complaints of pain and were thus insufficient to raise a triable issue of fact. Moreover, plaintiffs offered no competent medical proof that directly substantiated the claim that Uddin could not perform substantially all his daily tasks for 90 of the first 180 days due to an injury or impairment caused by the accident. Although Dr. DiGiancinto's affirmation attempted to substantiate this claim medically, he had no personal knowledge of Uddin's medical condition in early 2001. Inasmuch as he relied on unsworn medical reports from such period, they were hearsay and thus not probative of the issue. *Uddin v. Cooper.*

Accident victim wins. Notably, the report of the defendants' orthopedist specified the degrees of the range of motion in the plaintiff's cervical spine without comparing these findings to the normal range of motion. Thus, the defendants' proof failed to objectively demonstrate that the plaintiff did not suffer a permanent consequential or significant limitation of use of his cervical spine as a result of the subject accident. Since the defendants failed to establish, prima facie, their entitlement to judgment as a matter of law, the sufficiency of the papers in opposition need not be considered. *Aronov v. Leybovich.*

Accident victim wins. The defendants made a prima facie showing that the plaintiff James Bravo (hereinafter the injured plaintiff) did not sustain a serious injury within the meaning of Insurance Law § 5102(d) as a result of the subject motor vehicle accident. However, contrary to the determination of the Supreme Court, the affirmation of the injured plaintiff's treating physician, submitted in opposition to the defendants' motion for summary judgment, was sufficient to raise a triable issue of fact. The injured plaintiff's physician set forth the range of motion tests that he utilized, quantified the results of those tests, and concluded that the injured plaintiff sustained a significant consequential loss and limitation of motion in the cervical and lumbar spines. In addition, the physician's findings of decreased sensation over the right L4 and L5 dermatomes were corroborated by the findings of the defendants' neurologist. *Bravo v. Uvaydov.*

Accident victim wins. The defendants failed to establish that the plaintiffs did not sustain a serious injury within the meaning of Insurance Law § 5102(d) as a result of the subject accident. The defendants' examining orthopedic surgeon, who examined each of the plaintiffs on October 26, 2004, set forth in his affirmed medical reports his findings with respect to their ranges of motion in their cervical and lumbar spines, but failed to compare those findings to what is normal. Moreover, the defendants' examining neurologist, who examined the plaintiffs on November 10, 2004, merely stated in her reports that upon examination "movements of the neck are normal in all directions" without setting forth the objective testing used to arrive at those conclusions. Since the defendants failed to establish, prima facie, their entitlement to judgment as a matter of law, the sufficiency of the papers in opposition need not be considered. *Benitez v. Mileski.*

I hope you've found this book interesting:

That's all I have to say for now. Following are the three Appendices referred to earlier in the book. Appendix "A" is New York's Statement of Client's Rights. Exhibit "B" is the two color medical drawings depicting disc injury and nerve damage. Appendix "C" is my law firm's sample doctor's affirmation, used successfully in opposing a defense motion for summary judgment seeking to have my client's case thrown out for failing to meet New York's No-Fault "serious injury" threshold.

If you have questions, I urge you to ask an attorney, preferably an attorney experienced in handling accident cases. Of course, it's always best not to have an accident in the first place. So drive safely and pay attention. Stay off the cell phone. And pretty please don't drive if you drink (or drug). I've never had a client who wouldn't prefer to have back their good health instead of money.

APPENDIX A

Statement of Client's Rights

1. You are entitled to be treated with courtesy and consideration at all times by your lawyer and the other lawyers and personnel in your lawyers office.

2. You are entitled to an attorney capable of handling your legal matter competently and diligently, in accordance with the highest standards of the profession. If you are not satisfied with how your matter is being handled, you have the right to withdraw from the attorney-client relationship at any time (court approval may be required in some matters and your attorney may have a claim against you for the value of services rendered to you up to the point of discharge).

3. You are entitled to your lawyer's independent professional judgment and undivided loyalty uncompromised by conflicts of interest.

4. You are entitled to be charged a reasonable fee and to have your lawyer explain at the outset how the fee will be computed and the manner and frequency of billing. You are entitled to

request and receive a written itemized bill from your attorney at reasonable intervals. You may refuse to enter into any fee arrangement that you find unsatisfactory. In the event of a fee dispute, you may have the right to seek arbitration: your attorney will provide you with the necessary information regarding arbitration in the event of a fee dispute, or upon your request.

5. You are entitled to have your questions and concerns addressed in a prompt manner and to have your telephone calls returned promptly.

6. You are entitled to be kept informed as to the status of your matter and to request and receive copies of papers. You are entitled to sufficient information to allow you to participate meaningfully in the development of your matter.

7. You are entitled to have your legitimate objectives respected by your attorney, including whether or not to settle your matter (court approval of a settlement is required in some matters).

8. You have the right to privacy in your dealings with your lawyer and to have your secrets and confidences preserved to the extent permitted by law.

9. You are entitled to have your attorney conduct himself or herself ethically in accordance with the Code of Professional Responsibility.

10. You may not be refused representation on the basis of race, creed, color, religion, sex, sexual orientation, age, national origin or disability.

APPENDIX B

Normal disc

Herniated disc

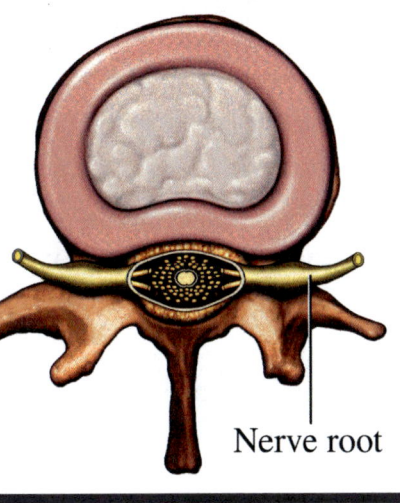

Nerve root

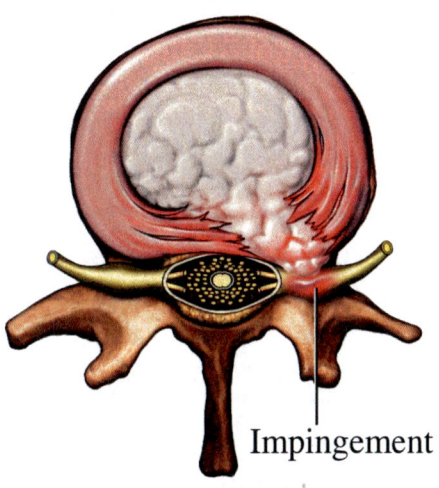

Impingement

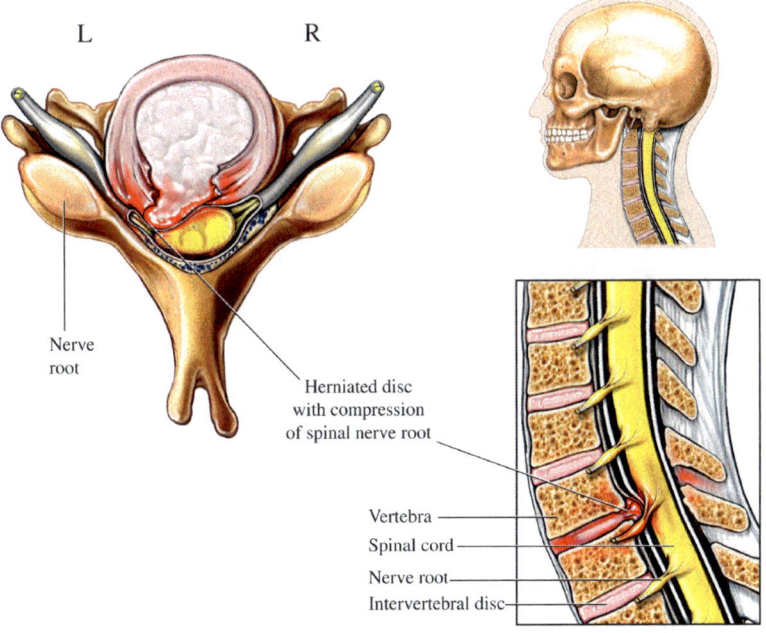

L   R

Nerve
root

Herniated disc
with compression
of spinal nerve root

Vertebra

Spinal cord

Nerve root

Intervertebral disc

APPENDIX C

A winning doctor's affidavit. See how: (a) the ranges of motion tests are described, (b) the normal ranges of motion are set down, (c) the accident victim's reduced ranges of motion are charted, (d) the accident victim's second, later accident is addressed, and, (e) it's important that he treated at the same medical facility for both accidents:

[Dr. K.], a physician duly licensed to practice medicine in the State of New York, affirms as follows under penalties of perjury:

1. I am a medical doctor and a Diplomate of the American Board of Physical Medicine & Rehabilitation. My office is located at [medical facility]. I have treated and tested [Accident Victim], and make this affirmation in support of the proposition that he has suffered a "serious injury," in excess of New York's No-Fault threshold.

FACTS

2. [Accident Victim] was involved in a motor vehicle accident on September 17, 1999 and one day after the accident, on September 18, 1999, he was seen at St. John's Hospital and admitted

until September 23, 1999. During this time, he underwent a cervical spine MRI on September 18, 1999 and a lumbar spine MRI on September 22, 1999. His hospital record, with MRI reports, is attached.

3. These MRI reports indicated: (a) a large left disc herniation at the C5-C6 level, extending into the proximal left C5-C6 neural foramen; (b) a herniated disc on the right and left sides of level C6-C7; (c) bony degenerative hypertropic changes with anterior osteophytes from the C4 level down through C7; and, (d) a mild increased signal intensity of the odontoid and the C3 and C6 vertebral bodies

4. These injuries to [Accident Victim]'s cervical discs are: (a) permanent; (b) painful; (c) injurious; and, (d) causally related to [Accident Victim]'s accident of September 17, 1999.

I HAVE REVIEWED THE MEDICAL FINDINGS AND TEST RESULTS OF [DR. W.] AND CONCUR WITH HIS FINDINGS

1. Approximately two weeks after being discharged from St. John's Hospital, [Accident Victim] sought treatment at [medical facility]. [Accident Victim] was first examined by [Dr. W.] on October 6, 1999.

2. I have reviewed the medical records and medical test results of [Dr. W.] dated October, 6, 1999, October 7, 1999, November 9, 1999, November 10, 1999, December 10, 1999, December 11, 1999, January 7, 2000, February 18, 2000, February 21, 2000 and March 13, 2000; and agree with his findings. The contents and substance of these reports is contained in [Accident Victim]'s chart, kept by my office in the regular course of business.

3. During medical examinations and objective medical testing, [Dr. W.] diagnosed [Accident Victim] with the following injuries: (a) post-traumatic headache; (b) post-traumatic vertigo; (c) cervical sprain/strain; (d) lumbar spine sprain/strain; (e) cervical radiculopathy; (f) lumbar radiculopathy; and, (g) trapezius muscle sprain/strain.

4. On December 8, 1999, [Dr. W.] performed a CPT (Current Perception Threshold) examination on [Accident Victim]. Testing exhibited: (a) a moderate hypoesthetic condition involving the left nerve root C6, (b) an advanced hypoesthetic condition involving the right nerve root C6 and left nerve root C7, (c) a very severe hypoesthetic condition involving the right nerve root C7, and, (d) a very mild sensory dysfunction in involving the left and right nerve root C8.

5. [Dr. W.] also conducted EMG/NCV examinations of the upper extremities and of the lower extremities on January 7, 2000. He diagnosed cervical radiculopathy at the level of bilateral C6-C7, more prevalent on the left, and lumbar radiculopathy at the level of bilateral S1, more prevalent on the left.

6. I wish to point out that the EMG tests nerve function electrically, through the insertion of needles into the muscle(s) served by the particular nerve(s) being tested, and by the application of a small electric current.

7. The EMG is widely recognized and accepted in the medical community as a diagnostic tool. It is considered an "objective" diagnostic test,

because the patient cannot willfully affect or "fake" the result, and is probably the best available or "gold standard" test of nerve function. Since the use of needles causes some discomfort to the patient, the EMG is only administered after a clinical examination elicits symptoms of nerve damage.

8. Muscle spasms are painful, involuntary muscle contractions often seen in skeletal muscle after acute injury. A muscle spasm cannot be released voluntarily and it is due to pain stimuli in the lower motor neuron. [Dr. W.] detected the presence of muscle spasms in [Accident Victim]'s lumbar and cervical paravertebral muscle. Spasm is an objective finding and cannot be faked.

9. The nerve damage detected by the CPT and EMG, and the muscle spasm, are: (a) permanent; (b) painful; (c) injurious; and, (d) causally related to [Accident Victim]'s accident of September 17, 1999.

I HAVE REVIEWED THE MEDICAL FINDINGS AND TEST RESULTS OF [DR. C-B.] AND CONCUR WITH HER FINDINGS

10. I have reviewed the medical records and medical test results of [Dr. C-B.] dated November 9, 1999, February 15, 2000, and February 22, 2001; and agree with her findings. The contents and substance of these reports is contained in [Accident Victim]'s chart, kept by my office in the regular course of business

11. [Accident Victim] was first examined by [Dr. C-B.] on November 9, 1999. During this initial physiatric examination, [Accident Victim] made complaints of back pain radiating to the right lower extremity with numbness and tingling of the right thigh; neck pain radiating to the left upper extremity with numbness and tingling of the left hand; and, headaches and dizziness.

12. [Accident Victim] was also treated by [Dr. C-B.] on February 15, 2000 and February 22, 2001 when he made similar complaints of pain. In addition to [Dr. W.]'s findings, [Dr. C-B.] also diagnosed [Accident Victim] with left lateral epicondylitis, post-concussion syndrome, and myofascial pain syndrome.

I HAVE REVIEWED THE MEDICAL FINDINGS AND TEST RESULTS OF [DR. D.] AND CONCUR WITH HIS FINDINGS

13. [Dr. D.], a neurologist at [medical facility] also treated [Accident Victim] for his 1999 accident. I have reviewed [Dr. D.]'s reports dated August 10, 2001 and October 29, 2001; and agree with his findings. The contents and substance of these reports is contained in [Accident Victim]'s chart, kept by my office in the regular course of business

14. In these reports, [Dr. D.] assessed residual symptoms of post-cerebral concussion syndrome and recurrent symptoms of cervical sprain, lumbar sprain, and cervical radiculopathy. He also detected decreased pin sensation over the left upper arm and forearm anterolaterally.

ALL THREE PHYSICIANS FOUND REDUCED RANGES OF MOTION

15. The three aforementioned physicians performed range of motion studies and quantified [Accident Victim]'s diminished ranges of motion as follows:

   a.   **NECK (CERVICAL SPINE):**
   (I) **Flexion:** Normal range of motion is 45 degrees.

Description of test: The patient is asked to bend the head forward so that the chin touches the chest. When the patient reaches the limit of the bending maneuver, the doctor observes the imaginary angle made by the cervical spine with an imaginary vertical line running through the thoracic spine. The appropriate imaginary angle is recorded.

Date tested	Physician testing	Range of motion found	Degree of loss	Percent of loss
10/6/99	[Dr. W.]	35°	10° loss	22%
11/9/99	[Dr. C-B.]	35°	10° loss	22%
12/10/99	[Dr. W.]	35°	10° loss	22%
2/15/00	[Dr. C-B.]	35°	10° loss	22%
2/18/00	[Dr. W.]	40°	5° loss	11%
8/10/01	[Dr. D.]	25°	20° loss	44%
10/29/01	[Dr. D.]	30°	15° loss	33%

(ii) **Extension:** Normal range of motion is 45 degrees.

Description of test: The patient is asked to bend the head backward, using the neck only, so that the eyes rest on the ceiling. When the cervical spine reaches the limit of the bending maneuver, the doctor measures the angle made by the cervical spine with the imaginary vertical line through the thoracic spine.

Date tested	Physician testing	Range of motion found	Degree of loss	Percent of loss
10/6/99	[Dr. W.]	35°	10° loss	22%
11/9/99	[Dr. C-B.]	30°	15° loss	33%
12/10/99	[Dr. W.]	35°	10° loss	22%
2/15/00	[Dr. C-B.]	35°	10° loss	22%
2/18/00	[Dr. W.]	35°	10° loss	22%
8/10/01	[Dr. D.]	10°	35° loss	78%
10/29/01	[Dr. D.]	20°	25° loss	56%

(iii) **Rotation**: Normal range of motion is 90 degrees.

Description of test: The patient is asked to stand or sit upright with the shoulders stationary, next to look toward each shoulder and then as far to the rear as possible. The doctor observes and records the angle in degrees made by the patient's head as it turns away from an imaginary horizontal line running through an axis of the nose between the two eyes as the patient looks straight ahead.

Date tested	Physician testing	Range of motion found	Degree of loss	Percent of loss
10/6/99	[Dr. W.]	35° bilaterally	55° loss	61%
11/9/99	[Dr. C-B.]	70° bilaterally	20° loss	22%
12/10/99	[Dr. W.]	35° bilaterally	55° loss	61%
2/15/00	[Dr. C-B.]	75° bilaterally	15° loss	17%
2/18/00	[Dr. W.]	35° bilaterally	55° loss	61%
8/10/01	[Dr. D.]	40°(right) 30°(left)	50° loss 60° loss	56% 67%
10/29/01	[[Dr. D.]	60°(right) 40°(left)	30° loss 50° loss	33% 56%

(iv) **Lateral Bending:** Normal range of motion is 45 degrees.

Description of test: The patient is asked to try to rest his or her ear on the shoulder, first to the right and then to the left. At the limit of this maneuver, the angle made by the cervical spine with the imaginary line running through the thoracic spine is recorded for both sides.

Date tested	Physician testing	Range of motion found	Degree of loss	Percent of loss
10/6/99	[Dr. W.]	35° bilaterally	10° loss	22%
11/9/99	[Dr. C-B.]	35° bilaterally	10° loss	22%
12/10/99	[Dr. W.]	35° on right 40° on left	10° loss 5° loss	22% 11%
2/15/00	[Dr. C-B.]	35° bilaterally	10° loss	22%
2/18/00	[Dr. W.]	35° on right 40° on left	10° loss 5° loss	22% 11%
8/10/01	[Dr. D.]	20°(right) 15°(left)	25° loss 30° loss	56% 67%
10/29/01	[Dr. D.]	30°(right) 20°(left)	15° loss 25° loss	33% 56%

b. BACK (LUMBAR SPINE):

(I) **Flexion**: Normal range of motion is 90 degrees.

Description of test: The patient is asked to bend over and attempt to touch the floor with the finger tips. With the patient's arms hanging loosely toward the floor, and with the knees straight and the feet together, the angle that the patient's trunk makes with an imaginary line running through the lower extremities is noted. In addition, or as an alternative, the distance from the patient's fingertips to the floor may be measured.

Date tested	Physician testing	Range of motion found	Degree of loss	Percent of loss
10/6/99	[Dr. W.]	75°	15° loss	17%
11/9/99	[Dr. C-B.]	70°	20° loss	22%
12/10/99	[Dr. W.]	75°	15° loss	17%
2/15/00	[Dr. C-B.]	30°	60° loss	67%
2/18/00	[Dr. W.]	75°	15° loss	17%
8/10/01	[Dr. D.]	50°	40° loss	44%
10/29/01	[Dr. D.]	40°	50° loss	56%

(ii) **Extension:** Normal range of motion is 30 degrees.

Description of test: With the feet together (the position of the hands and arms is immaterial), the patient is asked to bend backward. The doctor measures the angle made by the position of the back in extension and an imaginary line running through the patient's lower extremities.

Date tested	Physician testing	Range of motion found	Degree of loss	Percent of loss
10/6/99	[Dr. W.]	20°	10° loss	33%
11/9/99	[Dr. C-B.]	10°	20° loss	67%
12/10/99	[Dr. W.]	25°	5° loss	17%
2/15/00	[Dr. C-B.]	10°	20° loss	67%
2/18/00	[Dr. W.]	25°	5° loss	17%
8/10/01	[Dr. D.]	10°	20° loss	67%
10/29/01	[Dr. D.]	15°	15° loss	50%

(iii) **Rotation:** Normal range of motion is 45 degrees bilaterally.

Description of test: With the patient standing in an erect position with the feet together, the doctor observes the rotation of the lumbar spine as the patient turns the head and shoulders as far as possible, first in one direction and then in another. The range of shoulder motion, in degrees, is recorded by the examining physician.

Date tested	Physician testing	Range of motion found	Degree of loss	Percent of loss
10/6/99	[Dr. W.]	30° on right 35° on left	15° loss 10° loss	33% 22%
11/9/99	[Dr. C-B.]	35° bilaterally	10° loss	22%
12/10/99	[Dr. W.]	35° bilaterally	10° loss	22%
2/15/00	[Dr. C-B.]	20°	25° loss	56%
2/18/00	[Dr. W.]	35° bilaterally	10° loss	22%
8/10/01	[Dr. D.]	15°(right) 25°(left)	30° loss 20° loss	67% 44%
10/29/01	[Dr. D.]	15°(right) 10°(left)	30° loss 35° loss	67% 78%

(iv) **Lateral Bending (flexion):** Normal range of motion is 30 degrees to each side.

Description of test: The patient stands with the back to the doctor, who asks the patient to bend to the left and then to the right, keeping the feet

together and the legs straight, and with the hands
locked behind the head. Two observations are
made. The first is the smoothness of the motion; the
second is the actual range of side bending as
measured in degrees.

Date tested	Physician testing	Range of motion found	Degree of loss	Percent of loss
10/6/99	[Dr. W.]	20° bilaterally	10° loss	33%
11/9/99	[Dr. C-B.]	20° bilaterally	10° loss	33%
12/10/99	[Dr. W.]	25° bilaterally	5° loss	17%
2/15/00	[Dr. C-B.]	10° bilaterally	20° loss	67%
2/18/00	[Dr. W.]	25° bilaterally	5° loss	17%
8/10/01	[Dr. D.]	10°(right) 20°(left)	20° loss 10° loss	67% 33%
12/10/01	[Dr. D.]	20°(right) 15°(left)	10° loss 15° loss	33% 50%

1. These diminished ranges of motion are: (a)
   permanent; (b) painful; (c) injurious; and, (d)
   causally related to [Accident Victim]'s accident
   of September 17, 1999.

2. **[Dr. W.]** found, on October 6, 1999, diminished
   range of motion on straight leg raising with as
   much as a twenty degree loss on the right and a
   ten degree loss on the left during his medical
   examination and testing of [Accident Victim].
   Over the next four months, [Dr. W.] noted a
   slight improvement to this plane of motion on

the right (still diminished to ten degrees). Normal straight leg raising is to ninety degrees.

3. During his medical examinations and medical testing of [Accident Victim], [Dr. W.] also noted positive objective test results as follows:

(a) *Foraminal Compression Test*, which assesses any encroachment of the nerve roots in the neck area just to the side of their exit from the spinal cord. This test is indicated in patients who complain of pain that begins in the neck and radiates down the arm;

(b) *Kemp's Test*. During this test, the examiner stands behind the seated patient and bends the patient back at an oblique angle, first to one side and then to the other. If the patient feels pain on the side to which he or she is leaning, it indicates a medial disc protrusion; if pain is felt on the opposite side, it indicates a lateral protrusion;

(c) *L'Hermitte's Test*, a sensation similar to an electrical shock radiating from the back of the head, down the spine and into the limbs, is felt when the neck is bent forward.

4. [Dr. W.] also found that [Accident Victim] suffered from diminished pinprick and light touch and temperature sensation in the right C6 and left S1 dermatomal distribution.

5. Based on his medical examinations and medical testing, [Dr. W.] causally related [Accident Victim]'s complaints of pain and injuries to his accident of September 17, 1999.

6. **[Dr. C-B.]** found that [Accident Victim] suffered from diminished straight leg raising by twenty degrees on the right when examined on November 9, 1999. By [Dr. C-B.]'s physical examination on February 15, 2000, [Accident Victim]'s diminished straight leg raising had deteriorated to fifty degrees on the right. A loss of range of motion of approximately forty degrees (with normal straight leg raising at ninety degrees, bilaterally).

7. In her medical reports, [Dr. C-B.] also discusses her findings that [Accident Victim] suffered from cervical spine radiculopathy and lumbosacral spine radiculopathy.

8. **[Dr. D.]**, on August 10, 2001, assessed positive straight leg raising on the right at 20 degrees and on the left at 50 degrees was made. During

[Accident Victim]'s next visit of October 29, 2001, [Dr. D.] found positive straight leg raising at 30 degrees, bilaterally.

9. [Accident Victim] was involved in a subsequent (second) accident on November 26, 2001 and continued receiving medical treatment and testing at [medical facility] with [Dr. D.] and, later, with me.

10. During [Accident Victim]'s treatment for his subsequent accident, [Dr. D.] found that [Accident Victim] continued to suffer from diminished ranges of motion in his cervical and lumbosacral spine. [Dr. D.] concluded that [Accident Victim] still had residuals of neck and back pains which were aggravated by the subsequent (second) accident.

I AM CURRENTLY TREATING [ACCIDENT VICTIM]

11. During my initial examination of [Accident Victim], he complained of constant neck pain that radiated down the extent of his left upper extremity with numbness in his left arm. [Accident Victim] also complains of constant lower back pain.

12. Upon information and belief, [Accident Victim] had been out of work from the time of his September 17, 1999 accident until approximately one week prior to his November 26, 2001 accident.

13. During my initial medical examination and testing of [Accident Victim] I found additional injuries, including diminished ranges of motion in his upper extremities and positive objective testing. Since these are "new" injuries and not pre-existing I have not included my findings here since they are not relevant to show the exacerbation of [Accident Victim]'s injuries caused by the accident of September 17, 1999.

14. I conducted medical examinations and testing on [Accident Victim] and issued reports dated April 12, 2002, May 10, 2002, June 11, 2002, August 2, 2002, February 18, 2003, April 23, 2003, July 3, 2003, August 11, 2003, October 16, 2003, and February 19, 2004. I affirm that the contents of these reports are true and correct.

I FIND REDUCED RANGES OF MOTION

15. On April 12, 2002 and February 19, 2004 I performed range of motion testing on [Accident Victim]'s cervical spine and lumbosacral spine (this testing post-dates his subsequent accident of November 26, 2001, discussed below). I found as follows:

16.   a. **NECK (CERVICAL SPINE):**
     (I) **Flexion:** Normal range of motion is 45 degrees.

Date tested	Range of motion found	Degree of loss	Percent of loss
April 12, 2002	40°	5° loss	11%
February 19, 2004	40°	5° loss	11%

(ii)   **Extension**: Normal range of motion is 45 degrees.

Date tested	Range of motion found	Degree of loss	Percent of loss
April 12, 2002	15°	30° loss	33%
February 19, 2004	15°	30° loss	33%

(iii)   **Rotation**: Normal range of motion is 90 degrees.

Date tested	Range of motion found	Degree of loss	Percent of loss
April 12, 2002	45° Bilaterally	45° loss	67%
February 19, 2004	45° Bilaterally	45° loss	67%

(iv) **Lateral Bending**: Normal range of motion is 45 degrees.

Date tested	Range of motion found	Degree of loss	Percent of loss
April 12, 2002	40° Bilaterally	5° loss	11%

b. **BACK (LUMBAR SPINE):**

(I) **Flexion**: Normal range of motion is 90 degrees.

Date tested	Range of motion found	Degree of loss	Percent of loss
April 12, 2002	60°	30° loss	33%
February 19, 2004	60°	30° loss	33%

(ii) **Extension**: Normal range of motion is 30 degrees.

Date tested	Range of motion found	Degree of loss	Percent of loss
April 12, 2002	20°	10° loss	33%
February 19, 2004	20°	10° loss	33%

(iii) **Rotation**: Normal range of motion is 45 degrees bilaterally.

Date tested	Range of motion found	Degree of loss	Percent of loss
April 12, 2002	30° bilaterally	15° loss	33%

(iv) **Lateral Bending (flexion)**: Normal range of motion is 30 degrees to each side.

1. Additionally, [Accident Victim] continues to suffer from decreased sensation to light touch and pinprick in the left C5-C6 dermatomes. [Accident Victim]'s decreased sensation was pre-existing and exacerbated as a result of his accident of November 26, 2001.

2. As of my most recent examination on February 19, 2004, I diagnose [Accident Victim] with cervical radiculopathy, lumbar radiculopathy, cervical and lumbar disc herniation, myofascial pain syndrome, and muscle spasm.

3. Also, there are tender areas with taut bands in the bilateral paraspinals, right side worse than left, right quadratus, and the right gluteus medius; all taut bands are in a radiating pattern. There is also diminution to light touch and pin prick in the right upper thigh, lateral side.

CONCLUSION

4. My review of the medical records and test results of [Accident Victim] indicates that he suffered from diminished ranges of motion in his cervical spine, lumbar spine, cervical spine radiculopathy and lumbosacral radiculopathy for approximately a two year period from September 17, 1999 up until November 26,

2001, when [Accident Victim] was involved in a subsequent (second) accident.

5. [Accident Victim]'s first accident, the one here before the Court, left him with a permanent, partial disability. His second accident was the "icing on the cake," aggravating and exacerbating the injuries he suffered on September 17, 1999 and rendering him totally disabled.

6. Based on the medical information provided to me, including objective medical test results and my own medical examinations and objective medical testing, [Accident Victim] has suffered limited ranges of motion from September 17, 1999, the date of his first accident, for some five (5) years. The fact that the ranges of motion have remained reduced over such a lengthy period emphasizes the seriousness of [Accident Victim]'s injuries and indicate that these injuries are permanent.

7. Indication of the permanency of [Accident Victim]'s injuries is the consistency of the findings of diminished ranges of motion in his cervical spine and lumbosacral spine based on objective medical testing by numerous physicians over an extended period of time.

Many significant findings, made by clinical examination and by the numerous tests above discussed, to wit, CPT, MRI, EMG, range of motion, pre-existed his second accident.

8. The results stated in the MRI and EMG examinations of [Accident Victim], that is, the presence of cervical radiculopathy, lumbosacral radiculopathy and diminished sensation put together with the reduced range of motions and muscle spasms, are permanent injuries which have been caused by trauma from [Accident Victim]'s motor vehicle accident of September 17, 1999.

9. The spinal disc injury, the nerve damage, and restricted ranges of motion are all consistent with each other in establishing injury caused by the accident of September 17, 1999.

10. Based upon the history obtained, review of medical records and objective medical testing, clinical examination findings, and results of the EMG and MRI examinations, and the fact that injuries persist some five (5) years after the accident of September 17, 1999, it is my professional opinion that [Accident Victim] has sustained a permanent/partial disability and a permanent consequential limitation of use,

causally related to his motor vehicle accident of September 17, 1999.

Dated: Queens, New York
    April   , 2004

[signed: Dr. K.]